P9-DVZ-876

AFRICAN-AMERICANS IN BUSINESS

TISH DAVIDSON

TITLES IN THIS SERIES

AFRICAN-AMERICAN ACTIVISTS
AFRICAN-AMERICAN ARTISTS
AFRICAN-AMERICAN EDUCATORS
AFRICAN-AMERICAN MUSICIANS
AFRICAN-AMERICAN SCIENTISTS AND INVENTORS
AFRICAN-AMERICAN WRITERS AND JOURNALISTS
AFRICAN AMERICANS IN BUSINESS
AFRICAN AMERICANS IN LAW AND POLITICS
AFRICAN AMERICANS IN THE MILITARY
AFRICAN AMERICANS IN RADIO, FILM, AND TV ENTERTAINMENT
AFRICAN AMERICANS IN SPORTS
A HISTORY OF THE CIVIL RIGHTS MOVEMENT

AFRICAN-AMERICANS IN BUSINESS

TISH DAVIDSON

Mason Crest
Philadelphia

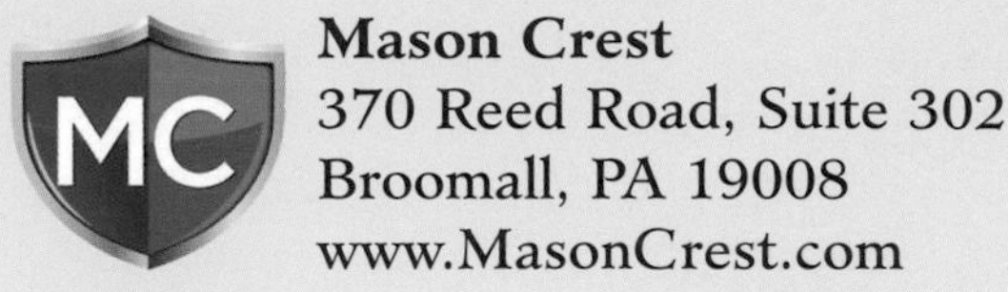

Mason Crest
370 Reed Road, Suite 302
Broomall, PA 19008
www.MasonCrest.com

Printed and bound in the United States of America.

CPSIA Compliance Information: Batch #MBC2012-7. For further information, contact Mason Crest at 1-866-MCP-Book.

First printing
1 3 5 7 9 8 6 4 2

Library of Congress Cataloging-in-Publication Data

Davidson, Tish.
African Americans in business / Tish Davidson.
p. cm. — (Major black contributions from emancipation to civil rights)
Includes bibliographical references and index.
ISBN 978-1-4222-2377-2 (hc)
ISBN 978-1-4222-2390-1 (pb)
1. African American business enterprises—History—Juvenile literature. 2. African American businesspeople—History—Juvenile literature. 3. Entrepreneurship—United States—History—Juvenile literature. I. Title.
HD2358.5.U6D38 2012
338.6'42208996073—dc23

2011051941

Publisher's note: All quotations in this book are taken from original sources, and contain the spelling and grammatical inconsistencies of the original texts.

Picture credits: Associated Press: 30; courtesy Daymond John: 12 (top); Getty Images: 20, 40; Time & Life Pictures/Getty Images: 49; Reuters/Shannon Stapleton /Landov: 16; Library of Congress: 3, 8, 10, 14, 18, 26, 28, 32, 33, 39, 42, 48; National Park Service: 21; North Carolina Mutual Life Insurance: 23; PR Newswire photo: 24; BET Networks/PR Newswire: 53; Radio One: 45; used under license from Shutterstock.com: 3, 35; Helga Esteb / Shutterstock.com: 46, 50; Albert H. Teich / Shutterstock.com: 12 (bottom); Derrick Salters / Shutterstock.com: 51; Joe Seer / Shutterstock.com: 52; Wikimedia Commons: 35 (inset).

TABLE OF CONTENTS

Introduction 6
by Dr. Marc Lamont Hill,
Institute for Research in African American Studies at Columbia University.

1 Overcoming Obstacles: Growing Black Businesses 9

2 Service Businesses: Personal Care, Funeral Homes, and Hospitality 13

3 Managing Money: Banking, Insurance, and Investment 19

4 Buying and Selling: Manufacturing, Distribution, and Sales 25

5 Building on the Land: Real Estate 31

6 Getting the News Out: Publishing................................ 39

7 Behind the Stars: Entertainment Businesses 47

Chapter Notes 54
Chronology 56
Glossary 58
Further Reading 60
Internet Resources 61
Index 62
Contributors 64

INTRODUCTION

Dr. Marc Lamont Hill

It is impossible to tell the story of America without telling the story of Black Americans. From the struggle to end slavery, all the way to the election of the first Black president, the Black experience has been a window into America's own movement toward becoming a "more perfect union." Through the tragedies and triumphs of Blacks in America, we gain a more full understanding of our collective history and a richer appreciation of our collective journey. This book series, MAJOR BLACK CONTRIBUTIONS FROM EMANCIPATION TO CIVIL RIGHTS, spotlights that journey by showing the many ways that Black Americans have been a central part of our nation's development.

In this series, we are reminded that Blacks were not merely objects of history, swept up in the winds of social and political inevitability. Rather, since the end of legal slavery, Black men and women have actively fought for their own rights and freedoms. It is through their courageous efforts (along with the efforts of allies of all races) that Blacks are able to enjoy ever increasing levels of inclusion in American democracy. Through this series, we learn the names and stories of some of the most important contributors to our democracy.

But this series goes far beyond the story of slavery to freedom. The books in this series also demonstrate the various contributions of Black Americans to the nation's social, cultural, technological, and intellectual growth. While these books provide new and deeper insights into the lives and stories of familiar figures like Martin Luther King, Michael Jordan, and Oprah Winfrey, they also introduce readers to the contributions of countless heroes who have often been pushed to the margins of history. In reading this series, we are able to see that Blacks have been key contributors across every field of human endeavor.

Although this is a series about Black Americans, it is important and necessary reading for everyone. While readers of color will find enormous purpose and pride in uncovering the history of their ancestors, these books should also create similar sentiments among readers of all races and ethnicities. By understanding the rich and deep history of Blacks, a group often ignored or marginalized in history, we are reminded that everyone has a story. Everyone has a contribution. Everyone matters.

The insights of these books are necessary for creating deeper, richer, and more inclusive classrooms. More importantly, they remind us of the power and possibility of individuals of all races, places, and traditions. Such insights not only allow us to understand the past, but to create a more beautiful future.

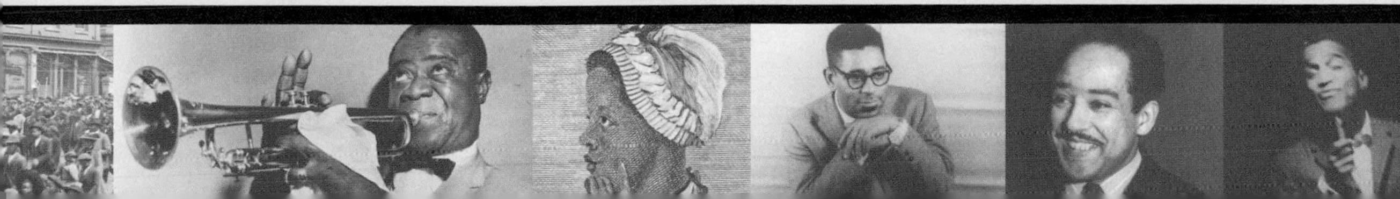

An African-American store owner stands in the doorway of his Harlem grocery, circa 1940; the sign above reads "Our Own Community Grocery & Delicatessen." For many years, businesses owned by African American were mostly limited to black customers, because many whites refused to buy their products or shop in their stores.

1

OVERCOMING OBSTACLES
GROWING BLACK BUSINESSES

Every day, African Americans start new businesses. As with all new businesses, many of them will fail. Some will grow for a while and then collapse. A few succeed beyond their founders' wildest expectations.

After the Civil War ended in 1865, African Americans had to build new social and business networks. Some newly freed blacks used skills they had learned as slaves to start businesses. But black entrepreneurs faced many obstacles. They often had little education or experience with business. Banks would not lend them money. Whites would not buy from them, and their African American customers were often so poor that business owners had to accept vegetables, eggs, and chickens from them instead of cash. African Americans also faced racism. Successful black enterprises were sometimes driven out of business by jealous whites using threats and force.

Between 1910 and 1915, there was a great migration of African Americans from farms in the South to cities in the North. More blacks in cities meant more customers for black businesses. In the South, segregation forced black people to use black-owned restaurants, stores, and services. In the North, white businesses made blacks feel unwelcome. Black-owned stores took advantage of this. One black-owned shop advertised itself as "a place where Negro ladies can . . . have their dresses fitted and be treated like ladies."

The Coleman Manufacturing Company in North Carolina (left) was the first cotton mill owned and operated by African Americans. It was started by Warren C. Coleman (right), who had been born a slave in 1850. After emancipation Coleman had attended college, then opened a successful store. The mill operated for about five years, but financial problems and Coleman's death in 1904 led to its closure.

The Great Depression ruined many American businesses, black and white, large, and small. Unemployment was high. People struggled to buy the basics—food, clothing, and shelter. But in the 1940s, World War II brought new jobs and better pay for African Americans as factories worked overtime to support the war effort. For companies that had survived the Depression, business began to improve.

THE COMING OF THE CIVIL RIGHTS MOVEMENT

The Civil Rights Movement that began in the mid-1950s brought a huge change to black businesses. The 1964 Civil Rights Act made it illegal to refuse to serve blacks at hotels and restaurants. Segregation began to ease. This was good for the race, but bad for black businesses. Many of their customers began to shop at white-owned stores and eat at white-owned restaurants.

At the same time, African Americans began getting better-paying jobs. They had more money to spend. The white business community noticed this and began targeting their advertising to black consumers.

The flow of dollars away from African-American businesses hurt the black community. The owners of successful black small businesses were likely to spend their profits in the communities where they lived. Money spent at white-owned businesses, on the other hand, usually did not return to the black community. Also, as customers went elsewhere many black-owned businesses had to close their doors. This meant that workers, most or all of whom were African Americans, lost their jobs.

A Company Destroyed by Racism

S. B. Fuller (1905–1988) grew up poor but with a can-do attitude. Like many other African Americans of his time, Fuller moved from the South to Chicago with almost no money. Driven by a desire to better himself, Fuller began selling soap door to door. His company grew and hired many sales people.

In 1947, Fuller bought a company that sold cosmetics to white women in the South. He said, "I have always believed that black producers should sell to white customers the same way whites sell to blacks." But he kept ownership of the company secret because he thought whites would not buy from his black-owned company. He was right. When white store owners learned that an African American owned the cosmetics company, they refused to carry his products, and he lost over half his profits.

Fuller had problems with the black community too. In a speech to the National Association of Manufacturers, Fuller said that a "lack of understanding of the capitalist system and not racial barriers was keeping blacks from making progress." This enraged civil rights leaders of the 1960s, and they encouraged African Americans stop buying Fuller's products. His company declared bankruptcy in 1972.

Daymond John (b. 1969) started the apparel company FUBU ("For us, by us") in 1992. Like many African-American entrepreneurs, he began working from home in his spare time, sewing hats. Within a few years, FUBU products were distributed around the world, with annual sales of more than $300 million. In 2010, the company changed its name to FB Legacy.

Federal affirmative action programs requiring that a certain percentage of contracts on public works projects be given to minority-owned businesses helped some companies through this difficult time. Most of these programs were phased out in the 1980s.

AFRICAN AMERICAN BUSINESS TODAY

Today, better educational opportunities, and anti-discrimination laws give African Americans more choice in how they participate in the business world. Many still open their own businesses, but others choose to enter the corporate world. A few have risen to the top of multi-million dollar corporations and serve as models for the next generation. Whichever path they take, African Americans entering business still need a good preparation, determination, and commitment to succeed.

Former business executive Herman Cain (b. 1945) used his experiences at CEO of Godfather's Pizza (1986–1996) and as head of the National Restaurant Association (1996–1999) to run as a candidate for president. He unsuccessfully sought the Republican Party's nomination for the 2012 election.

2

SERVICE BUSINESSES
PERSONAL CARE, FUNERAL HOMES, AND HOSPITALITY

Before the Civil War, a few free blacks had small businesses. These businesses usually provided wealthy whites with personal services such as barbering, hairdressing, dressmaking, and washing clothes. Barbershops were the most financially successful. For example, in 1830, free black William Johnson (1809–1851) of Natchez, Mississippi, owned three barbershops that took in about $300 each month (equal to about $7,000 today).

After the Civil War, most African American businesses continued to be service businesses. They usually were small and employed only a few people. African Americans had trouble getting the money to start or expand businesses, so the number of black businesses grew slowly.

BLACKS SERVING BLACKS

Funeral homes were among the first black businesses established specifically to meet the personal needs of African Americans. They succeeded because white funeral homes often refused to serve black people, and blacks felt more comfortable being buried by people who understood their traditions. In 1893, Lucy Jefferson (1866–1953) and her husband founded the W. H. Johnson Funeral Home. This was the first black-owned funeral home in Mississippi. It is still in business today.

Horses and carriages in front of the Chattanooga, Tennessee, funeral home operated by C.W. Franklin, an African-American undertaker, circa 1899.

Gertrude Geddes Willis (1878–1970) was one of the first women to become a funeral director in New Orleans. She married Clem Geddes, whose family owned a funeral home. When he died, Gertrude continued to run the business. She married again and reorganized the funeral home calling it the Gertrude Geddes Willis Funeral Home. Then she founded the Gertrude Geddes Willis Insurance Company. Her businesses made her a millionaire and one of the most important African-American women in New Orleans. Both the funeral home and the insurance company are still in business, and the tradition of black funeral homes continues today.

AFRICAN AMERICANS IN THE HOSPITALITY BUSINESS

Many whites thought that serving food and providing lodging was low-class work suitable only for servants. This attitude allowed African Americans to open inns, hotels, restaurants, and catering businesses without a lot of competition from whites.

Even before the Civil War, Philadelphia was the center of the black catering industry. Several families controlled catering in Philadelphia. One of the most successful was the Dutrieuille family. As a young man, Peter

Albert Dutrieuille (1838–1916) worked as a shoemaker. He became involved in catering when he married Amelia Baptiste, whose family owned a catering business. After spending nine years learning the business from Amelia's family, Dutrieuille started his own catering company. In time, Dutrieuille's son Albert (1877–1974) took over from his father. The company stayed in business until Albert Dutrieuille died.

Peter Dutrieuille also helped organize the Caterers Manufacturing and Supply Company. This was an African American cooperative company. The company bought tables, chairs, dishes, and silverware. Caterers who joined the company could rent these items whenever they needed them. Sharing equipment saved the caterers money. Caterers Manufacturing and Supply is an example of how African Americans worked together to help each other succeed in business.

Caterers also thrived in other cities. In New York, twelve black caterers formed the Corporation of Caterers to protect their business interests and prevent "irresponsible men from attempting to cater at weddings, balls, parties." In Washington, one black entrepreneur used profits from his catering to build a splendid hotel.

Did You Know?

George T. Downing (1819–1903) ran the restaurant for the United States House of Representatives from 1865 to 1877. He was an early civil rights leader. At age 14, he organized a boycott of the Fourth of July to protest that the Declaration of Independence's promise of liberty for all did not include African Americans. In Washington, Downing worked unsuccessfully for passage of an early civil rights bill and served as vice president of the National Negro Labor Union.

FROM CATERING TO HOTELS

James Wormley (1819–1884) was truly an international man. He was born to free black parents in Washington D.C. His first job was driving a carriage for his father's carriage rental business. Soon bored with this, he took a job

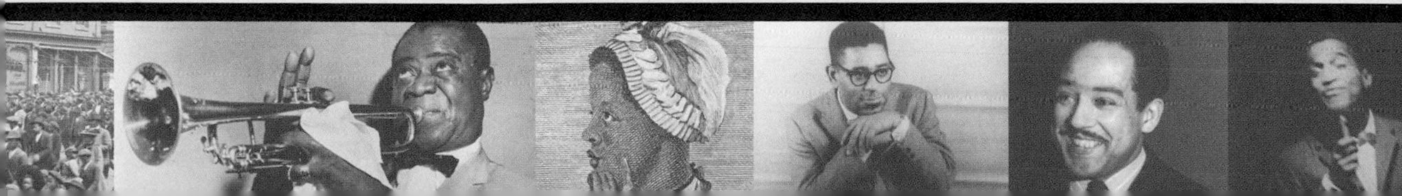

Sylvia Woods, Queen of "Soul Food"

The term "soul food" was created in the 1960s to describe food traditionally eaten by African-Americans in the South. Interest in soul food arose from the black pride movement of the 1960s that encouraged African Americans to honor their heritage.

In 1962, Sylvia Woods (b. 1926) bought a tiny luncheonette in Harlem and named it Sylvia's Restaurant. Here she cooked the food she had eaten growing up in South Carolina: fried chicken, ham hocks, grits, collard greens, black-eyed peas, and sweet potato pie. Her business grew. She moved Sylvia's into a larger restaurant, started a catering business, and published several cookbooks. A *New York Times* restaurant reviewer called Sylvia Woods "the undisputed queen of soul food." By the 1990s, people were coming from all over the world to eat her cooking.

Sylvia Woods stands outside the Harlem landmark Sylvia's Restaurant during its 40th anniversary celebration, 2002.

as steward on a ship. In 1848, when gold was discovered in California, he went west hoping to strike it rich. He did not find gold, so he returned to Washington, D.C., and started a catering business and restaurant.

Wormley's restaurant was popular with politicians in Washington. One of them, Reverdy Johnson, became the ambassador to England. Johnson asked Wormley to go with him to England as his steward. Here Wormley learned about preparing fine food and serving politically powerful people.

After taking cooking classes in France, Wormley returned to Washington and opened the stylish Wormley Hotel. At the time it was the only hotel in Washington owned and operated by an African American. Soon Wormley's hotel became a meeting place for politicians and important visitors from foreign governments. Wormley was unusual in the hotel business because he was a black man whose hotel served important white people. He died a millionaire in 1884.

Did You Know?

Janet Bragg (1907–1993) was the first African American woman to own an airplane and obtain a commercial pilot license. Because of gender and race discrimination, she could not earn a living as a pilot, so she opened a nursing home.

Nursing was a way for African American women to move up in status and out of domestic service. Often nursing was done through individual private arrangements between the client and the nurse, but some African American women like Janet Bragg established successful health care businesses.

SEGREGATION, INTEGRATION, AND THE HOSPITALITY BUSINESS

Until the late 1950s, restaurants and hotels, especially in the South, were segregated by race. Segregated accommodations made it difficult for African Americans to travel. In 1943, there were only 529 black-owned hotels in the entire United States. However, the policy of "separate but equal" was good for black hotel, motel, and restaurant owners because it forced black people to use their services.

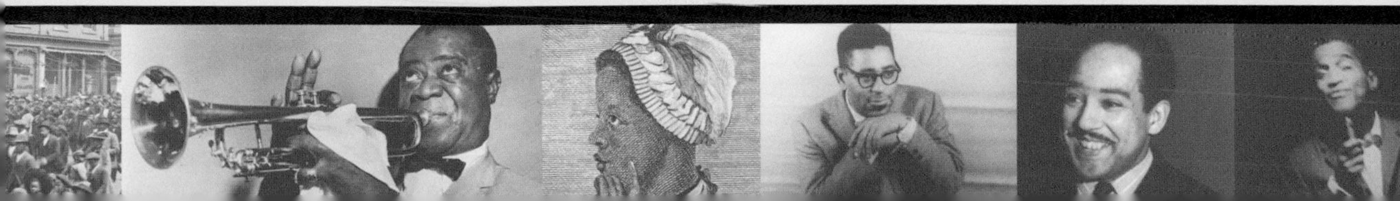

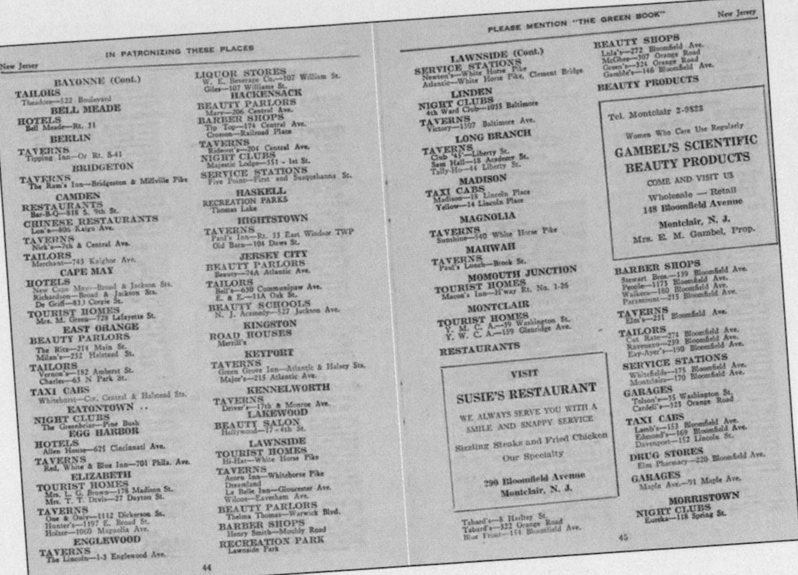

IN PATRONIZING THESE PLACES

New Jersey

BAYONNE (Cont.)

TAILORS
Theodore—522 Boulevard

BELL MEADE

HOTELS
Bell Meade—Rt. 31

BERLIN

TAVERNS
Tipping Inn—Or Rt. S-41

BRIDGETON

TAVERNS
The Ram's Inn—Bridgeton & Millville Pike

CAMDEN

RESTAURANTS
Bar-B-Q—818 S. 9th St.

CHINESE RESTAURANTS
Lee's—806 Kaign Ave.

TAVERNS
Nick's—7th & Central Ave.

TAILORS
Merchant—743 Kaighns Ave.

CAPE MAY

HOTELS
New Cape May—Broad & Jackson Sts.
Richardson—Broad & Jackson Sts.
De Griff—833 Corgie St.

TOURIST HOMES
Mrs. M. Green—728 Lafayette St.

EAST ORANGE

BEAUTY PARLORS
The Ritz—214 Main St.
Milan's—232 Halstead St.

TAILORS
Vernon's—182 Amherst St.
Charles—63 N Park St.

TAXI CABS
Whitehurst—Cor. Central & Halstead Sts.

EATONTOWN

NIGHT CLUBS
The Greenbriar—Pine Brush

EGG HARBOR

HOTELS
Allen House—625 Cincinnati Ave.

TAVERNS
Red, White & Blue Inn—701 Phila. Ave.

ELIZABETH

TOURIST HOMES
Mrs. L. G. Brown—178 Madison St.
Mrs. T. T. Davis—27 Dayton St.

TAVERNS
One & Only—1112 Dickerson St.
Hunter's—1197 E. Broad St.
Holder—1060 Magnolia Ave.

ENGLEWOOD

TAVERNS
The Lincoln—1-3 Englewood Ave.

LIQUOR STORES
W. E. Beverage Co.—107 William St.
Giles—107 Williams St.

HACKENSACK

BEAUTY PARLORS
Mary—206 Central Ave.

BARBER SHOPS
Tip Top—174 Central Ave.
Cromon—Railroad Place

TAVERNS
Rideout's—204 Central Ave.

NIGHT CLUBS
Majestic Lodge—351 - 1st St.

SERVICE STATIONS
Five Point—First and Susquehanna St.

HASKELL

RECREATION PARKS
Thomas Lake

HIGHTSTOWN

TAVERNS
Paul's Inn—Rt. 33 East Windsor TWP
Old Barn—104 Dews St.

JERSEY CITY

BEAUTY PARLORS
Beauty—74A Atlantic Ave.

TAILORS
Bell's—630 Communipaw Ave.
E. & E.—11A Oak St.

BEAUTY SCHOOLS
N. J. Academy—527 Jackson Ave.

KINGSTON

ROAD HOUSES
Merrill's

KEYPORT

TAVERNS
Green Grove Inn—Atlantic & Halsey Sts.
Major's—215 Atlantic Ave.

KENNELWORTH

TAVERNS
Driver's—17th & Monroe Ave.

LAKEWOOD

BEAUTY SALON
Hollywood—17 - 4th St.

LAWNSIDE

TOURIST HOMES
Hi-Hat—White Horse Pike

TAVERNS
Acorn Inn—Whitehorse Pike
Dreamland
La Belle Inn—Gloucester Ave.
Wilson—Evesham Ave.

BEAUTY PARLORS
Thelma Thomas—Warwick Blvd.

BARBER SHOPS
Henry Smith—Mouldy Road

RECREATION PARK
Lawnside Park

44

PLEASE MENTION "THE GREEN BOOK" New Jersey

LAWNSIDE (Cont.)

SERVICE STATIONS
Newton's—White Horse Pike
Atlantic—White Horse Pike, Clement Bridge

LINDEN

NIGHT CLUBS
4th Ward Club—1035 Baltimore

TAVERNS
Victory—1307 Baltimore Ave.

LONG BRANCH

TAVERNS
Club "45"—Liberty St.
Sam Hall—18 Academy St.
Tally-Ho—44 Liberty St.

MADISON

TAXI CABS
Madison—18 Lincoln Place
Yellow—14 Lincoln Place

MAGNOLIA

TAVERNS
Sunshine—340 White Horse Pike

MAHWAH

TAVERNS
Paul's Lunch—Brook St.

MOMOUTH JUNCTION

TOURIST HOMES
Macon's Inn—H'way Rt. No. 1-26

MONTCLAIR

TOURIST HOMES
Y. M. C. A.—39 Washington St.
Y. W. C. A.—159 Glenridge Ave.

RESTAURANTS

VISIT
SUSIE'S RESTAURANT
WE ALWAYS SERVE YOU WITH A SMILE AND SNAPPY SERVICE
Sizzling Steaks and Fried Chicken Our Specialty
290 Bloomfield Avenue
Montclair, N. J.

Tabard's—8 Harley St.
Tabard's—322 Orange Road
Blue Front—114 Bloomfield Ave.

BEAUTY SHOPS
Lula's—272 Bloomfield Ave.
McGhee—307 Orange Road
Green's—324 Orange Road
Gamble's—146 Bloomfield Ave.

BEAUTY PRODUCTS

Tel. Montclair 2-9823
Women Who Care Use Regularly
GAMBEL'S SCIENTIFIC BEAUTY PRODUCTS
COME AND VISIT US
Wholesale — Retail
148 Bloomfield Avenue
Montclair, N. J.
Mrs. E. M. Gambel, Prop.

BARBER SHOPS
Stewart Bros.—139 Bloomfield Ave.
People—1173 Bloomfield Ave.
Walkers—180 Bloomfield Ave.
Paramount—215 Bloomfield Ave.

TAVERNS
Elm's—231 Bloomfield Ave.

TAILORS
Cut Rate—274 Bloomfield Ave.
Ravenezo—239 Bloomfield Ave.
Eay-Ayer's—190 Bloomfield Ave.

SERVICE STATIONS
Whitefields—175 Bloomfield Ave.
Montclair—170 Bloomfield Ave.

GARAGES
Tolson's—35 Washington St.
Cardell's—323 Orange Road

TAXI CABS
Lamb's—153 Bloomfield Ave.
Edmond's—169 Bloomfield Ave.
Davenport—152 Lincoln St.

DRUG STORES
Elm Pharmacy—220 Bloomfield Ave.

GARAGES
Maple Ave.—91 Maple Ave.

MORRISTOWN

NIGHT CLUBS
Eureka—118 Spring St.

45

The *Negro Motorist Green Book* was a travel guide that identified and reviewed hotels and restaurants open to African Americans in the United States, and later in Canada, Mexico, and Bermuda. The guide was created by a Harlem businessman named Victor H. Green, and was published annually from 1936 to 1964. These pages are from the 1949 edition.

During the 1940s, more African Americans could afford cars and vacations. Many black hotel owners provided simple rooms for travelers. But a few built luxury resorts to attract wealthy blacks. In 1942, Sally Walker started building a resort in the Catskill Mountains in New York. By 1954, her all-black resort included a lodge, private cabins, several dining rooms and dance floors, a casino, a lake for swimming, basketball and tennis courts, and a golf course. A newspaper article at the time reported that it was "not rare to see in her mail requests for reservations from vacationists in Europe."

In the mid-1950s, white business people realized that they could make money by building hotels and motels for African Americans. These accommodations were still segregated, but they competed with black-owned lodging. Then in 1964, the Civil Rights Act was passed. It outlawed racial discrimination in public accommodations. As white hotels, motels, and restaurants gradually accepted black customers, many black-owned food and lodging establishments went out of business.

3

MANAGING MONEY
BANKING, INSURANCE, AND INVESTMENT

Before the Civil War, there were no banks or insurance companies for African Americans. But the black community developed two organizations that served some of the same purposes: burial societies and mutual aid societies.

Having a proper funeral was important to most African Americans. A person who joined a burial society regularly paid small amounts of money to the society. When that person died, the burial society paid for the funeral. This was an early form of insurance.

Mutual aid societies were similar to burial societies. People regularly paid small amounts of money into a fund. Then, if a member got or sick or died, the mutual aid society used money from the fund to help the family. Some mutual aid societies also acted like banks and made loans to their members.

THE FIRST BLACK-OWNED BANKS

After the Civil War, the government set up the Freedman's Savings and Trust, a bank run by whites for African Americans. The bank was badly managed. It went out of business in 1874. At that time, the government did not insure bank deposits the way it does today. African Americans who had opened accounts at the bank lost all their money.

Customers wait in line at the Dunbar National Bank in Harlem, 1933. Advertisements published when the bank opened in 1928 noted that it had been "established particularly to serve the business and personal banking interests of Harlem's Negro population."

About the time the Freedman's bank failed, William Washington Browne (1849–1897) started the United Order of the True Reformers in Alabama. This was a temperance, or anti-alcohol, organization run as a mutual aid society. Browne was an inspiring leader who started many branches of the True Reformers.

In 1880, Browne moved his organization's headquarters to Richmond, Virginia. Next, he made each True Reformer pay $1.50 (about $33 in today's dollars) to join. In exchange, the member's family received $100

($2,200 today) when the member died. To make this work, Browne needed to invest the membership money. In 1888, Virginia allowed him to start the True Reformers Bank. This was the first truly black-owned-and-operated bank in the United States. The bank made money by buying and selling real estate and making loans to its members. Unfortunately, the bank failed 13 years after Browne died, when one of its employees stole $50,000 (more than $1.1 million today) from it.

AN AFRICAN-AMERICAN WOMAN BANKER

Maggie Lena Walker (1867–1934) of Richmond, Virginia, was the first woman of any race to become a bank president. Her father was murdered when she was young. Her mother worked doing people's laundry, but she insisted that Maggie graduate from high school. During high school, Maggie joined the Independent Order of St. Luke, a mutual aid society. She eventually became the leader of the Order and increased its membership. By the 1920s, eight out of every ten African Americans in Richmond belonged to the Order.

Maggie Lena Walker was a remarkable entrepreneur. She started a bank, a newspaper, and a store nearly two decades before American women gained the right to vote.

As membership grew, Walker followed William Browne's lead and started the St. Luke Penny Savings Bank. Walker's bank encouraged people to open accounts even if they could only save small amounts. She told them the bank "will take nickels and turn them into dollars." Walker especially wanted to help African-American women. She hired them to work in the bank, at the Order's headquarters, and at a newspaper and department store that she started. Unlike

many banks at that time, her bank made loans to women so that they could buy their own homes.

In the 1930s, Walker's bank joined with two other banks and became the Consolidated Bank and Trust Company. It is still in business in Virginia today. In 1978, Maggie Walker's house in Richmond became a National Historic Site and is open to visitors.

THE RISE OF BLACK INSURANCE COMPANIES

White life insurance companies did not want to insure black people. They thought African Americans were too much of a risk "because of social diseases, living conditions, and other undesirable circumstances." This

A Modern Black-Owned Bank

In 1992, Emma Chappell (b.1941) became the first black woman to found a bank since Maggie Walker. After high school Chappell began working as a clerk for Continental Bank in Philadelphia. By going to night school, she earned a degree from Temple University and qualified for an executive training program at the bank. In time, she became a Continental Bank vice president.

Chappell wanted to help the black community. The bank where she worked made very few loans to minorities. So in 1987, some black business leaders asked Chappell to found a black-controlled bank specifically to help the African American community. Five years later, United Bank of Philadelphia opened with Chappell as CEO. The bank made a special effort help small African American business owners and poor people who had never before had bank accounts.

Chappell served as the bank's CEO until 2000. The bank continues to operate in the Philadelphia area today.

encouraged mutual aid societies to start insurance programs. In 1905, Joseph Edison Walker (1880–1958), a doctor who was not related to Maggie Walker, moved to Indianola, Mississippi. Here he met Wayne Cox, a wealthy African American. Cox started the Delta Penny Savings Bank and the Mississippi Life Insurance Company. Walker soon became president of the bank and later president of the insurance company.

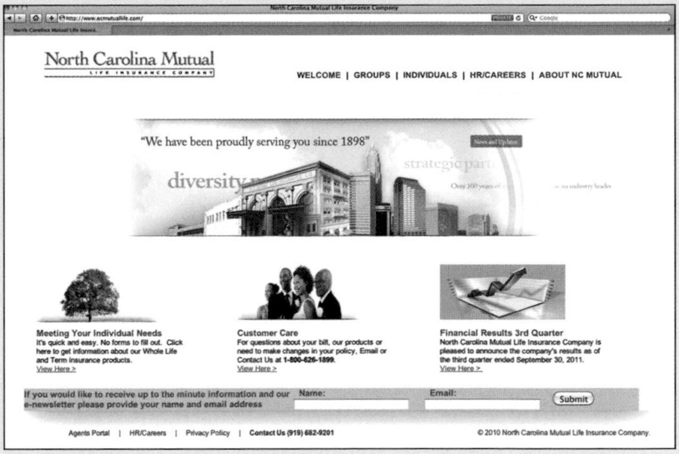

John Merrick and Aaron Moore founded North Carolina Mutual Life Insurance in 1898. Charles Spaulding (1874–1952) started working there in 1900 as a part-time insurance salesman, clerk, and janitor. Twenty-three years later, he was president of the company. Spaulding believed that money paid by African Americans for insurance should be invested in projects such as hospitals and libraries for the African-American community. His philosophy was successful. North Carolina Mutual Life Insurance is still in business today.

In the early 1900s, there was extreme racial discrimination in Indianola. Whites were especially angry at successful blacks such as Cox and Walker. For this reason, Walker moved the Mississippi Life Insurance Company to Memphis, Tennessee. In Memphis, Mississippi Life had trouble competing against half a dozen other black insurance companies. Eventually economic war among these black companies allowed Mississippi Life to be taken over by a white company. Walker and a group of black business leaders then started Universal Life Insurance Company in 1923.

After a few difficult years, Universal Life became a successful company. Joseph Walker's son, Antonio Maceo Walker, joined the business and became president in 1952. He helped expand and modernize Universal Life and started the Tri-State Bank. Walker's customers were all black. His biggest complaint was "whites simply don't trade with blacks in business . . . My two businesses just simply can't develop like they should, 'cause

I've got no white trade." Despite this, Universal Life and Tri-State Bank are still in business.

INTEGRATING FINANCIAL COMPANIES

The Civil Rights Movement of the 1960s increased the number of African Americans college graduates going to work in previously all-white financial companies. Kenneth Chenault's career is typical. Chenault (b. 1951) graduated from Bowdoin College in Maine and earned a law degree from Harvard in 1976. After working as a management consultant for five years, he took a job at American Express Company. During the next twenty years, Chenault was promoted into more and more responsible jobs. In 2001, he became the chief executive officer (CEO) of the entire company, a position he held for more than 10 years.

Kenneth Chenault

Stanley O'Neal (b. 1951), the grandson of a former slave, grew up to become CEO of Merrill Lynch, a $50 billion investment bank. Until he was 13, O'Neal lived in poverty on a small family farm in Alabama. He explained his childhood this way. "We had little. No car, no running water or indoor toilets. But I was lucky because I had parents who knew it was important for me to go to school." In 1986, having earned a graduate degree from Harvard Business School, O'Neal went to work for Merrill Lynch. Eventually, he held the position of CEO from 2002 to 2007.

Although blacks have been making progress in modern financial companies, racial discrimination still happens. In 1991, Alphonse Fletcher, Jr. (b. 1966), another Harvard graduate, sued his employer Kidder, Peabody & Company. He claimed the financial firm discriminated against him and failed to pay him what he had been promised. Fletcher won the payment part of the suit, but lost the discrimination part. Fletcher then started his own company, Fletcher Asset Management. The success of this firm has allowed him to give generously to the National Association for the Advancement of Colored People (NAACP) and to support other African American educational causes.

4

BUYING AND SELLING
MANUFACTURING, DISTRIBUTION, AND SALES

For years after Emancipation, most African Americans were poor. Because they had little money, white manufacturers did not consider black preferences in the products they made and sold. This left an opening for black entrepreneurs to make products specifically for the African American community. However, by the 1950s, white companies began to compete with black-owned businesses in selling black-oriented products.

MADAME C. J. WALKER

Hair care and cosmetics were the first and most successful black-oriented products made by African Americans. The most successful hair care entrepreneur was Sarah Breedlove (1867–1919), better known as Madame C. J. Walker. Breedlove was born into a poor farming family in Louisiana. She was orphaned at age seven, married at 14, a mother at 18, and widowed at 20. After her husband's death, Breedlove moved to St. Louis. For the next 18 years she worked doing laundry.

Chemicals from the laundry made Breedlove's hair fall out, so she began experimenting with ways to grow her hair back. According to her,

Portrait of Madame C.J. Walker, who has been called the first self-made female millionaire.

the correct hair formula came to her in a dream. "A big black man appeared to me and told me what to mix up for my hair. Some of the remedy was grown in Africa, but I sent for it, mixed it, put it on my scalp, and in a few weeks my hair was coming in faster than it had ever fallen out . . . I made up my mind to sell it."

A SUCCESSFUL SALES PROGRAM

Breedlove started selling her hair formula door to door in St. Louis but soon moved to Denver, Colorado. There she married C. J. Walker. For the rest of her life, she called herself Madame C. J. Walker.

Walker's business strategy was to train other women in the Walker Method of hair care. These women then sold Walker's products door to door. Women who sold large amounts were rewarded with trips and jewelry. One former Walker sales agent explained, "People would want to become agents and learn the trade so that they could travel. They found out that they could make money plus have a new way of getting away from home." By 1910, 5,000 black women were selling Walker's products.

Walker was ambitions, hard working, and strong willed. She opened a manufacturing plant in Indianapolis, divorced her husband over business differences, became a millionaire, and donated generously to causes that helped African American women.

Other African American entrepreneurs followed Walker's lead. Sarah Washington

(1889–1953) became a millionaire by establishing beauty schools and selling cosmetics from her base in Atlantic City, New Jersey. Anthony Overton (1865–1946) manufactured and distributed hair care products and cosmetics, extending his sales overseas to Africa. George Johnson (b. 1927) had phenomenal success with his hair straightening products until the 1960s, when the natural Afro look became popular.

A BLACK BUSINESS SELLING TO WHITES

In 1992, *Black Enterprise* magazine declared the James Produce Company

Annie Turnbo-Malone

Some people think Madame C. J. Walker made millions by copying the formula and sales methods of Annie Turnbo-Malone (1869–1957). Turnbo-Malone sold homemade "Wonderful Hair Grower" in St. Louis in the early 1900s. She trained women to sell her product door to door. Later she claimed that Walker had worked for her. It is not clear whether this is true, but Walker did use many of the same sales techniques as Turnbo-Malone.

Turnbo-Malone went on to establish the Poro cosmetics company. Poro College, her training center, had classrooms, an auditorium, restaurants, and guest rooms. It became a center of black social life in St Louis. By 1924, Turnbo-Malone was a millionaire.

Turnbo-Malone's business started to fall apart in 1927 when her husband demanded control of Poro as part of a divorce settlement. Although he did not get control of the company, Turnbo-Malone had to pay him a $200,000 ($2.5 million today) cash settlement.

After the divorce, Poro's profits declined due to poor management, increased competition, and the Great Depression. Turnbo-Malone caused some of her own problems by refusing to pay taxes. She was sued many times by the government and by some of her employees. By the time she died, Turnbo-Malone had lost almost all of her property and savings.

African-American fruit and vegetable vendors attempt to sell their wares on a street in Richmond, Virginia, circa 1908.

as the oldest black businesses in America. Four generations of the James family have run this company.

In 1883, four James brothers began traveling around West Virginia selling small household items to farmers. Many farmers had no cash, so the brothers took eggs and vegetables as payment. They sold this food to hotels and restaurants in Charleston. West Virginia had a small black population, so from the beginning, most of their customers were white. The family philosophy was “business is business, and race has no business in business.”

Over time, three brothers dropped out of the business, leaving it to Charles Howell James (1862–1929). Then Charles’s son Edward (1983–1967) came to work for his father. Soon, instead of trading for vegetables, the company was buying them from nearby states and to sell to restaurants. Edward took complete control of the business in 1928.

DISASTER AND RECOVERY

The stock market crash of 1929 and the depression that followed almost killed the James family business. The company was in debt, and Edward had to declare bankruptcy. The man who had grown up in a big house with servants and plenty of money lost everything. Fortunately, Edward's wife got a job running the local post office. Using her income, Edward started a small roadside vegetable stand. Through hard work he rebuilt the family business. By 1957 he owned a large warehouse and later added a freezer so that he could sell frozen foods.

— Did You Know? —

Naomi Sims (b. 1949) became the first superstar black model in 1967. But modeling was not her career goal. She wanted to own a business. Her first company sold wigs for black women. Later she started Naomi Sims Beauty Products for African-American women.

When Edward died, his two sons took over, and in 1983 Edward's grandson joined the company. By that time James Produce had grown into a multi-million dollar food distribution business.

FROM THE STREETS TO HOLLYWOOD

Almost anyone who knew Wallace Amos (b. 1936) as a teenager would have predicted that he would never amount to much. Amos lived in Florida with his parents until he was 12. When his parents divorced, he was sent to New York to live with his aunt. He had a hard time making the change. Amos dropped out of school, ran away from home, lived on the streets, and gambled money stolen from his aunt. Eventually he pulled himself together and joined the Air Force.

After leaving the Air Force, Amos worked part time at Saks Fifth Avenue department store in New York. Impressed with his abilities, Saks

Wally Amos poses in the doorway of his Kailua, Hawaii, cookie shop with a hot batch of cookies, 2007. While building the Famous Amos cookie brand, Amos turned his store openings into extravagant events. Many celebrities came. Newspapers wrote about the opening and how the stars loved Famous Amos cookies. They were called "the superstar of cookies."

sent him to a management trainee course, but he dropped out because of his difficulty with math.

His next job was with William Morris Talent Agency. Starting in the mailroom, he worked his way up to assistant talent agent. In this job he booked musical acts like the Supremes and Temptations.

Realizing that he had risen as high as a black man could at William Morris, Amos left and went to Los Angeles. Here he worked with little success on the fringes of the music business. This was a low period in his life. Remembering his aunt's chocolate chip cookie recipe, Amos began baking cookies and handing them out with his business card in an attempt to get noticed. One day a record executive's secretary proposed that she and Amos go into the cookie business together. She suggested the name Famous Amos Cookies.

Amos had no money, but he knew people in the music business and persuaded some of them to invest in his cookie company. He was an excellent salesman and used his celebrity connections to market his cookies. By 1979 he was selling 7,000 pounds of chocolate chip cookies every day.

Wally Amos sold the company in 1985, but continued to work as its spokesman. He later started three other companies, wrote several bestselling books, and became a respected motivational speaker. Today, Famous Amos cookies are sold all over the world, earning more than $60 million each year.

5

BUILDING ON THE LAND
REAL ESTATE

For ex-slaves, owning a home and land provided security, respect, and a sign of success. Early in 1865, as Union armies captured areas of Confederate territory, newly freed black slaves were often given land where they could start their own farms, a policy known as "40 acres and a mule." At the end of the war, however, this policy ended.

Between 1863 and 1913, the number of black-owned homes rose from 9,000 to 555,000, and the number of black-owned farms increased from 20,000 to 937,000. Increased interest in property ownership opened up opportunities for African American land speculators, developers, and real estate agencies.

ISAIAH MONTGOMERY AND MOUND BAYOU

Isaiah Montgomery (1827–1924) was raised in Davis Bend, Mississippi, and educated with the plantation owner's children. Davis Bend was unusual. The white owner, Joseph Davis, encouraged black self-government and allowed his slaves to open their own businesses. Benjamin Montgomery (1819–1877), Isaiah's father, became the plantation's business manager. Isaiah became Davis's personal secretary.

A GENERAL VIEW OF MOUND BAYOU, SHOWING THE RAILROAD STATION

In the foreground, on the right, are Isaiah T. Montgomery and the town constable

returned to the plantation and in 1866 put himself in communication with Mr. Davis. Very soon they had perfected plans with him for the purchase of the Hurricane and Brierfield plantations, containing something like 4,000 acres of land, upon which the elder Montgomery and his sons, under the name of Montgomery & Sons, conducted the third largest plantation in the state.

It was the desire of Joseph Davis, after the war, to keep together as far as possible the slaves who had grown up on his plantations. His notion was, no doubt, that the interests of all concerned demanded that there should be just as little break in the old relations as possible and that the transition from slavery to freedom should be made gradually, with the idea that the freedmen should, however, eventually become the owners of the land upon which they had previously been slaves. The plantations were conducted with this end in view until 1880, when it became apparent to the Montgomerys that unless there was a modification of the terms upon which the project had been left to them after Joseph Davis's death, it would be impossible to succeed. The heirs could not agree to an alteration in terms, and so the scheme was finally abandoned.

It was with the same notion of carrying out, under new conditions, the plan which his father and his former master had formed years before, that, in 1887, Mr. Montgomery—as he says in a brief autobiography—"sought to begin anew, at the age of forty, the dream of life's young manhood," the dream of doing something to build up the fortunes of his race. It thus appears that the history of Mound Bayou is deeply rooted in the past, and is, in a certain sense, a carrying out of the scheme formulated by the elder Montgomery and his former master for the welfare of that master's former slaves. Others than were intended have become heirs to the plans of these men,

THE BANK OF MOUND BAYOU

ONE OF THE PRINCIPAL STORES

After the Civil War, Davis sold his plantation to the Montgomery family. They were to pay for it over time with the profits made from growing cotton. At first the plan worked. But later, bad weather, insect damage, and low cotton prices meant that they could not repay the loan. They lost the plantation in 1881.

With his father dead and the plantation gone, Isaiah Montgomery decided to found an all-black town. This was one of more than 100 all-black towns established between 1865 and 1915. Some towns were founded by speculators for profit. Others were founded by idealists who believed all-black towns were the only way for African Americans to escape discrimination. Isaiah Montgomery founded Mound Bayou, Mississippi, for both reasons.

In 1885, Montgomery and his cousin, Ben Green, bought 840 acres of swampy land between Memphis, Tennessee, and Vicksburg, Mississippi. After clearing the land, they advertised for settlers. By February 1888, Montgomery had sold 700 acres at $7 per acre. Most of the land was bought on credit, and Montgomery held the mortgages. Montgomery also owned a cotton gin, lumberyard, and general store and was mayor of Mound Bayou.

(Opposite) This page from the July 1907 issue of *The World's Work*, a monthly magazine, shows images of Mound Bayou, Mississippi. They accompanied an article titled "A Town Owned by Negroes," which called Mound Bayou "an example of thrift and self-government." Isaiah T. Montgomery is pictured at the top of the page with the town constable near the railroad station; the bottom photos show the town's bank and a store. (Right) Residents of Mound Bayou stand in front of the general store, circa 1940.

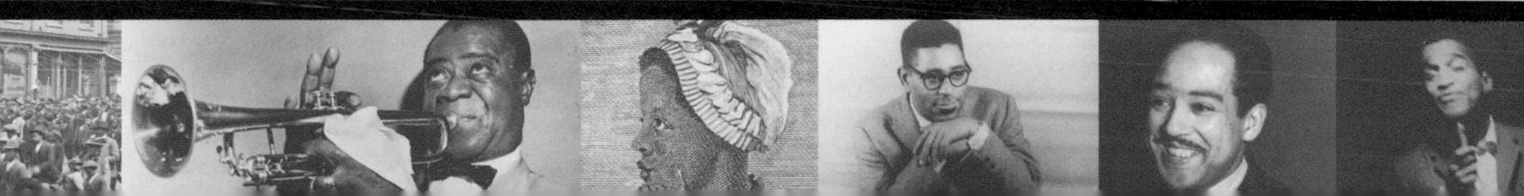

At first, cotton farmers in Mound Bayou prospered. But hard economic times in the 1920s eventually caused many people to leave Mound Bayou for cities like St. Louis, Chicago, and New York. Today Mound Bayou is home to about 2,000 people; 98.5 percent of them are African Americans.

THE ALLENSWORTH EXPERIMENT

Allen Allensworth (1842–1916) was born a slave in Louisville, Kentucky. At age 12, he was sold to a man from New Orleans. Here he worked as a racehorse jockey. During the Civil War, Allensworth joined the Union Navy. After the war he became a Baptist minister. He joined the United States Army as its first African-American chaplain.

After serving twenty years in the Army, Allensworth settled in Los Angeles. He was inspired by Booker T. Washington's teachings that African Americans should be help themselves, help each other, and become self-sufficient. Allensworth thought the best way to do this was to form an all-black town. In 1908, Allensworth and his business partner, William Payne, bought 800 acres of land about 30 miles north of Bakersfield, California. They laid out a town, sold lots, and within seven years the town they called Allensworth had 300 residents.

But several setbacks occurred. In 1914, Allen Allensworth was hit by a motorcycle and killed. That same year, the Santa Fe Railroad opened a new line that enabled trains to bypass the town. This deprived local businesses of revenue from travelers and railroad workers. This was a conscious decision on the part of the railroad's management. They had never supported the black community, and refused to hire African Americans to work at the train depot there. Finally, the underground water supply needed for farming began to dry up. By 1945, the town had disappeared. However, in 1976, California turned the town site of Allensworth into a state park.

A BLACK COMMUNITY IN NEW YORK

The Harlem area of Manhattan has not always been a black community. In the late 1890s it was an upscale segregated neighborhood for white people.

Real estate entrepreneur Philip A. Payton, Jr. (inset) became known as the "Father of Black Harlem" due to his work renting properties in the Harlem neighborhood of New York City to African Americans.

Beginning about 1900, real estate developers built many luxury apartment buildings on the edge of Harlem, thinking that more wealthy whites would move there. But these apartments were too expensive, and no one rented them. The developers could not repay the money they had borrowed, and they lost the apartment buildings to foreclosure. At the same time, large numbers of African Americans were moving to New York City. Philip Payton (1876–1917) saw a way to make money from these two events.

Philip Payton was born in Massachusetts and moved to New York after graduating from Livingstone College in North Carolina in 1899. He had trouble finding work but eventually got a job as a janitor at a real estate

office. After watching others make money in real estate, he decided to open the Afro-American Realty Company specializing in managing apartment buildings for black tenants.

At first Payton did so little business that he was evicted from two offices for nonpayment of rent. The turning point came when a white landlord who was in a dispute with another white landlord asked Payton to manage his apartment building and rent to blacks.

After this success, Payton found partners to invest in his business. He

Jesse Binga and the Great Migration

During the Great Migration between 1910 and 1930, 4.1 million African Americans left their farms and homes in the South to settle in cities in the North. These people needed a place to live. Jesse Binga (1865–1950) began buying up run-down houses in the black section of Chicago. He fixed them up and rented them to the new arrivals.

In Chicago, neighborhoods were segregated by race. With so many black families arriving from the South, the black neighborhoods became crowded. Binga bought buildings in white neighborhoods. Then he would move a black family into an all-white apartment building. The white families did not want to live near blacks. They would move out, and Binga would move more black families in, charging them higher rents than the white families had paid. This was called "block busting." It angered white residents so much that Binga's properties were bombed five times.

Block busting opened up new neighborhoods to African Americans in Chicago and made Binga rich, but Binga angered many blacks for charging very high rents.

Later Binga founded the Binga State Bank. The bank failed. People lost their savings, and Binga went to prison for three years for stealing from the bank. After he got out of prison, Binga worked as a church janitor and died a poor man.

began buying up the foreclosed luxury buildings in Harlem and renting the apartments to middle and upper class black families. At one point, Payton controlled twenty Harlem apartment buildings and was one of the richest black landlords in the country. White families quickly moved out of Harlem and by the 1920s Harlem had become the center of black arts and culture. Unfortunately, conflict among the investors in the Afro-American Realty Company destroyed the business, although Payton continued to work in real estate on a smaller scale.

Did You Know?

In an effort to keep neighborhoods all white, many banks would redline African American customers. *Redlining* is a discriminatory practice that occurs when banks refuse to lend minority borrowers money to buy homes in white neighborhoods even though the borrowers have good credit and qualify for the loan. Although redlining was made illegal in 1977, the practice still occasionally occurs today.

FIGHTING REAL ESTATE DISCRIMINATION

John Nail (1883–1947) and Henry Parker were employees of Philip Payton's Afro-American Realty Company. When they saw the company was being torn apart by a power struggle, they left to form their own real estate company. Nail was active in helping to break down an unwritten rule or "covenant" that certain blocks of Harlem would remain all white. He fought the banks that reinforced this covenant by redlining African Americans who wanted to buy homes on those blocks.

In time, Nail became a highly respected real estate agent. He handled a $200,000 property deal for Madame C. J. Walker and managed the largest apartment building in Harlem for the white-owned Metropolitan Insurance Company. Nail was also known for his support of African American business and cultural organizations, both nationally and in Harlem.

A young newsboy sells copies of the *Chicago Defender*, 1942. During its heyday, from about 1915 to 1950, the *Defender* was one of the most widely circulated and influential newspapers reporting on the African-American community.

6

GETTING THE NEWS OUT
PUBLISHING AND THE MEDIA

For years, the African American community remained almost invisible to white media companies. Many cities had large black populations, but mainstream newspapers reported almost no news about African Americans unless they were accused of a crime. As a result, black entrepreneurs stepped in fill the gap.

First came black-oriented newspapers, then magazines. Although these publications reported on everyday events in the African American community, they also played a major role in the fight for equality and civil rights. Some of these newspapers were distributed nationally and had great influence.

ROBERT ABBOTT AND THE DEFENDER

Robert Sengstacke Abbott (c.1868–1940) established what would become the first nationally distributed black-owned newspaper, the *Chicago Defender*. Abbott was born on San Simeon Island, Georgia. His father died soon after he was born, and his stepfather, Robert Sengstacke, became the major influence in his life. Sengstacke was a minister who published a small community newspaper. From him, Abbott learned about the newspaper business.

Through his newspaper, Robert S. Abbott fought for greater rights for African Americans. The *Chicago Defender* publicized and condemned instances of racial prejudice, and argued that blacks deserved to be considered for jobs and government positions.

After graduating from Hampton Institute, Abbott moved to Chicago. When he had difficulty finding a job, he went to law school. Upon graduation, the ebony-skinned Abbott was discouraged from practicing law when another African American lawyer told him he was "a little too dark to make any impression on the courts in Chicago." After this, Abbott turned to the skills he had learned at his stepfather's newspaper.

The *Defender* was born in May 1905. Abbott printed 300 copies on credit and sold them by going to black churches and clubs. The weekly paper remained small and struggled financially for the next few years.

THE DEFENDER BECOMES A NATIONAL PAPER

The *Defender*'s breakthrough as a national paper came after a new editor convinced Abbott to take a very aggressive position on race discrimination. At the same time, Abbott came up with a plan to distribute his newspaper to distant cities. White postal officials in many Southern cities and communities refused to deliver the *Defender*, so Abbott enlisted African-American men who worked as porters on railroad sleeping cars. They smuggled bundles of newspapers onto trains traveling south. The porters made sure to get them into African-American communities throughout the South. By 1916, the *Defender* was sold in 71 cities.

The effect of national distribution on the African Americans outside Chicago can be seen in the *Defender*'s Great Northern Drive. Abbott thought blacks should leave the South and to move north where there was less discrimination. *The Defender* printed story after story urging families make this move. The result was that more than 60,000 African Americans poured into Chicago in less than four years.

Following Abbott's death in 1940, his nephew John Sengstacke (1912–1997) took over the business. Sengstacke Publishing bought almost a dozen black newspapers including the *New York Age* and the *Pittsburgh Courier*. In 1980, it was one of the top 75 black businesses in America. However, increased reporting on the African American community by mainstream newspapers and the rise of the Internet has diminished the influence of black papers.

Black newspapers still serve the African American community. Today papers such as the *Defender*, the *Amsterdam News*, and the *Philadelphia Tribune* have established Web sites for their readers.

ALL THE NORMAL THINGS IN LIFE

When John Harold Johnson (1918–2005) started *Ebony Magazine* in 1945, he said he wanted to "show not only white people but also Negroes got married, had beauty contests, gave parties, ran successful businesses, and did all the normal things of life." *Ebony* was not Johnson's first magazine, and publishing was not his first career, but it was his most successful.

John Johnson was born in Arkansas and raised in Chicago. His first job was with Supreme Liberty Life Insurance, one of the most important black businesses in Chicago in the 1930s. Here he became assistant editor of the com-

Did You Know?

Earl Graves (b.1935) founded *Black Enterprise Magazine* to promote African American businesses and show that African Americans could be successful entrepreneurs. Each year the magazine publishes a list of the top 100 black-owned companies in America.

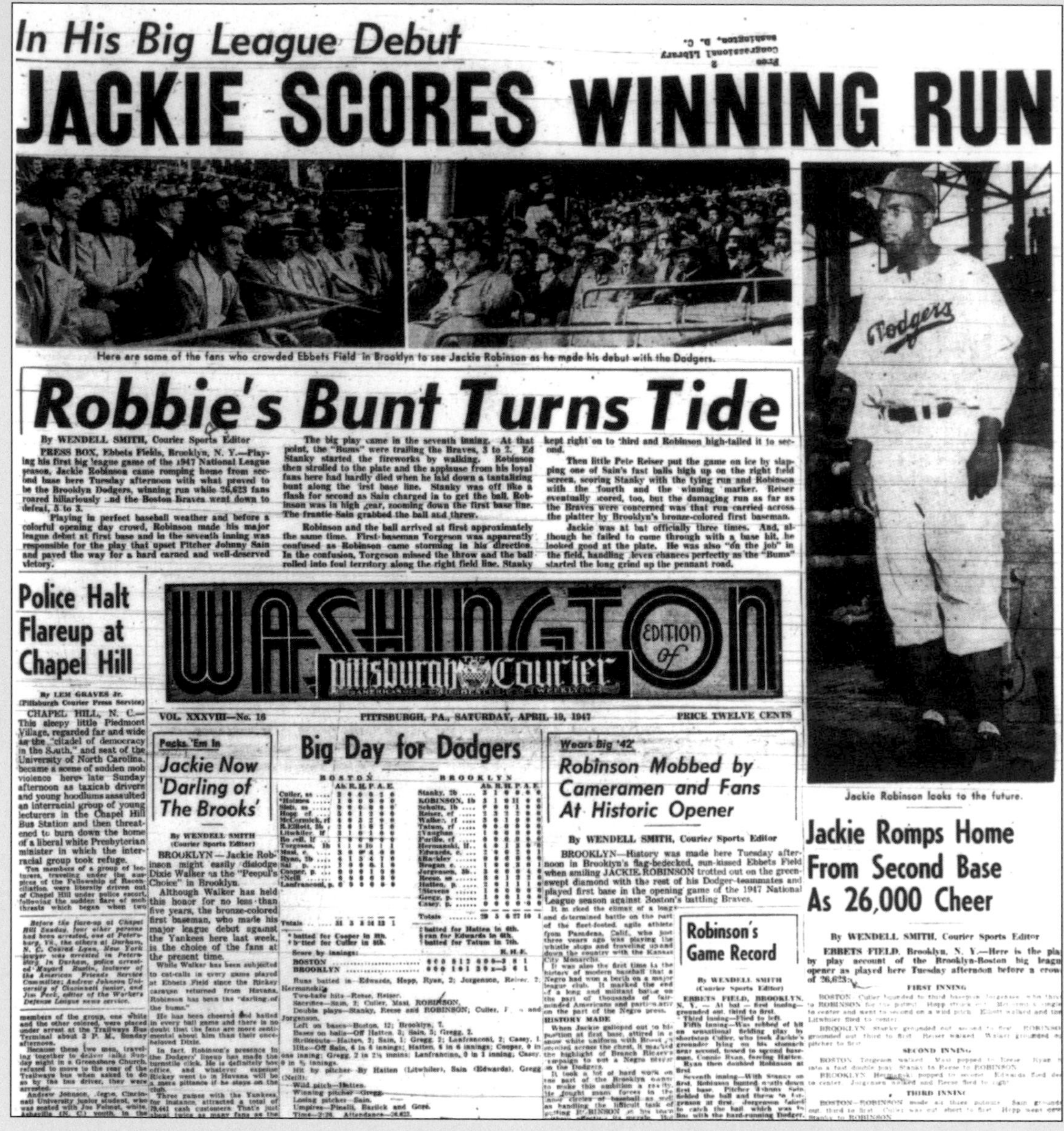

In His Big League Debut

JACKIE SCORES WINNING RUN

Here are some of the fans who crowded Ebbets Field in Brooklyn to see Jackie Robinson as he made his debut with the Dodgers.

Robbie's Bunt Turns Tide

By WENDELL SMITH, Courier Sports Editor

PRESS BOX, Ebbets Fields, Brooklyn, N. Y.—Playing his first big league game of the 1947 National League season, Jackie Robinson came romping home from second base here Tuesday afternoon with what proved to be the Brooklyn Dodgers, winning run while 26,623 fans roared hilariously and the Boston Braves went down to defeat, 5 to 3.

Playing in perfect baseball weather and before a colorful opening day crowd, Robinson made his major league debut at first base and in the seventh inning was responsible for the play that upset Pitcher Johnny Sain and paved the way for a hard earned and well-deserved victory.

The big play came in the seventh inning. At that point, the "Bums" were trailing the Braves, 3 to 2. Ed Stanky started the fireworks by walking. Robinson then strolled to the plate and the applause from his loyal fans here had hardly died when he laid down a tantalizing bunt along the first base line. Stanky was off like a flash for second as Sain charged in to get the ball. Robinson was in high gear, zooming down the first base line. The frantic Sain grabbed the ball and threw.

Robinson and the ball arrived at first approximately the same time. First-baseman Torgeson was apparently confused as Robinson came storming in his direction. In the confusion, Torgeson missed the throw and the ball rolled into foul territory along the right field line. Stanky kept right on to third and Robinson high-tailed it to second.

Then little Pete Reiser put the game on ice by slapping one of Sain's fast balls high up on the right field screen, scoring Stanky with the tying run and Robinson with the fourth and the winning marker. Reiser eventually scored, too, but the damaging run as far as the Braves were concerned was that run carried across the platter by Brooklyn's bronze-colored first baseman.

Jackie was at bat officially three times. And, although he failed to come through with a base hit, he looked good at the plate. He was also "on the job" in the field, handling seven chances perfectly as the "Bums" started the long grind up the pennant road.

Police Halt Flareup at Chapel Hill

By LEM GRAVES Jr.
(Pittsburgh Courier Press Service)

CHAPEL HILL, N. C.—This sleepy little Piedmont Village, regarded far and wide as the "citadel of democracy in the South," and seat of the University of North Carolina, became a scene of sudden mob violence here late Sunday afternoon as taxicab drivers and young hoodlums assaulted an interracial group of young lecturers in the Chapel Hill Bus Station and then threatened to burn down the home of a liberal white Presbyterian minister in which the interracial group took refuge.

Ten members of a group of lecturers, traveling under the auspices of the Fellowship of Reconciliation, were literally driven out of Chapel Hill under police escort, following the sudden flare of mob threats which began when two

Before the flare-up at Chapel Hill Sunday, four other persons had been arrested, one at Petersburg, Va., the others at Durham, N. C. Conrad Lynn, New York lawyer was arrested in Petersburg. In Durham, police arrested Bayard Rustin, lecturer of the American Friends Service Committee; Andrew Johnson University of Cincinnati junior, and Jim Peck, editor of the Workers Defense League news service.

members of the group, one white and the other colored, were placed under arrest at the Trailways Bus Terminal about 2 P. M. Sunday afternoon.

Because these two men, traveling together to deliver talks Sunday night in a Greensboro Church, refused to move to the rear of the Trailways bus when asked to do so by the bus driver, they were arrested.

Andrew Johnson, Negro, Cincinnati University junior student, who was seated with Joe Felmet, white, Asheville (N. C.) youth, in the

WASHINGTON EDITION of Pittsburgh Courier

VOL. XXXVIII—No. 16 PITTSBURGH, PA., SATURDAY, APRIL 19, 1947 PRICE TWELVE CENTS

Packs 'Em In

Jackie Now 'Darling of The Brooks'

By WENDELL SMITH
(Courier Sports Editor)

BROOKLYN—Jackie Robinson might easily dislodge Dixie Walker as the "Peepul's Choice" in Brooklyn.

Although Walker has held this honor for no less than five years, the bronze-colored first baseman, who made his major league debut against the Yankees here last week, is the choice of the fans at the present time.

While Walker has been subjected to cat-calls in every game played at Ebbets Field since the Rickey caravan returned from Havana, Robinson has been the "darling of the bums."

He has been cheered and hailed in every ball game and there is no doubt that the fans are more sentimental about him than their once-beloved Dixie.

In fact, Robinson's presence in the Dodgers' lineup has made the turnstile click. He is definitely box office, and whatever expense Rickey went to in Havana will be a mere pittance if he stays on the club.

Three games with the Yankees, for instance, attracted a total of 79,441 cash customers. That's just about twice as many fans as the

Big Day for Dodgers

BOSTON	Ab.	R.	H.	P.	A.	E.
Culler, ss	2	0	0	0	1	0
*Holmes	1	0	0	0	0	0
Sisti, ss	0	0	0	0	0	0
Hopp, cf	5	0	1	2	0	0
McCormick, rf	4	0	2	2	0	0
R.Elliott, 3b	2	0	1	0	2	0
Litwhiler, lf	3	1	0	1	0	0
Rowell, lf	1	0	0	0	0	0
Torgeson, 1b	4	1	0	10	1	1
Masi, c	3	0	0	4	0	0
Ryan, 2b	4	1	3	4	1	0
Sain, p	1	0	0	0	1	0
Cooper, p	0	0	0	1	0	0
†Neill	0	0	0	0	0	0
Lanfranconi, p	0	0	0	0	0	0
Totals	31	3	8	24	13	1

* batted for Cooper in 8th.
† batted for Culler in 8th.

BROOKLYN	Ab.	R.	H.	P.	A.	E.
Stanky, 2b	2	1	0	0	0	0
ROBINSON, 1b	3	1	0	11	0	0
Schultz, 1b	0	0	0	1	0	0
Reiser, cf	2	2	2	2	0	0
Walker, rf	3	0	1	0	0	0
Tatum, rf	0	0	0	0	0	0
‡Vaughan	1	0	0	0	0	0
Furillo, cf	0	0	0	0	0	0
Hermanski, lf	4	0	1	3	0	0
Edwards, c	2	0	0	2	0	1
§Rackley	0	0	0	0	0	0
Bragan, c	1	0	0	3	0	1
Jorgensen, 3b	3	0	0	0	4	0
Reese, ss	3	0	1	3	2	0
Hatten, p	2	0	1	1	1	0
¶Stevens	1	0	0	0	0	0
Gregg, p	1	0	0	1	0	0
Casey, p	0	0	0	0	0	0
Totals	29	5	6	27	10	1

‡ batted for Hatten in 6th.
§ ran for Edwards in 6th.
¶ batted for Tatum in 7th.

Score by innings:		R.	H.	E.
BOSTON	000 012 000—3		8	1
BROOKLYN	000 101 30x—5		6	1

Runs batted in—Edwards, Hopp, Ryan, 2; Jorgenson, Reiser, 2; Hermanski.
Two-base hits—Reese, Reiser.
Sacrifice—Sain, 2; Culler, Masi, ROBINSON.
Double plays—Stanky, Reese and ROBINSON; Culler, [illegible] and Jorgenson.
Left on bases—Boston, 12; Brooklyn, 7.
Bases on balls—Off Hatten, 3; Sain, 5; Gregg, 2.
Strikeouts—Hatten, 2; Sain, 1; Gregg, 2; Lanfranconi, 2; Casey, 1.
Hits—Off Sain, 6 in 6 innings; Hatten, 6 in 6 innings; Cooper, 0 in one inning; Gregg, 2 in 2⅓ innings; Lanfranconi, 0 in 1 inning; Casey, 0 in ⅓ innings.
Hit by pitcher—By Hatten (Litwhiler), Sain (Edwards), Gregg (Neill).
Wild pitch—Hatten.
Winning pitcher—Gregg.
Losing pitcher—Sain.
Umpires—Pinelli, Barlick and Gore.
Time—2:26. Attendance—26,623.

Wears Big '42'

Robinson Mobbed by Cameramen and Fans At Historic Opener

By WENDELL SMITH, Courier Sports Editor

BROOKLYN—History was made here Tuesday afternoon in Brooklyn's flag-bedecked, sun-kissed Ebbets Field when smiling JACKIE ROBINSON trotted out on the green-swept diamond with the rest of his Dodger-teammates and played first base in the opening game of the 1947 National League season against Boston's battling Braves.

It marked the climax of a long and determined battle on the part of the fleet-footed, agile athlete from Pasadena, Calif., who just three years ago was playing the whistle stops and traveling up and down the country with the Kansas City Monarchs.

It was also the first time in the history of modern baseball that a Negro had won a berth on a major league club. It marked the end of a long and militant battle on the part of thousands of fair-minded Americans and particularly on the part of the Negro press.

HISTORY MADE

When Jackie galloped out to his position at first base, attired in a snow white uniform with Brooklyn emblazoned across the chest, it marked the highlight of Branch Rickey's campaign to put a Negro player on the Dodgers.

It took a lot of hard work on the part of the Brooklyn owner to make this ambition a reality. He fought many forces in the inner circles of baseball as well as handling the difficult task of putting ROBINSON at his ...

Robinson's Game Record

By WENDELL SMITH
(Courier Sports Editor)

EBBETS FIELD, BROOKLYN, N. Y. — At bat — first inning—grounded out, third to first.

Third inning—Flied to left.

Fifth inning—Was robbed of hit on sensational fielding play by shortstop Culler, who took Jackie's grounder lying on his stomach near second, tossed to second baseman, Connie Ryan, forcing Hatten.

Ryan then doubled Robinson at first.

Seventh inning—With Stanky on first, Robinson bunted neatly down first base. Pitcher Johnny Sain fielded the ball and threw to Torgeson at first. Jorgeson failed to catch the ball which was in line with the hard-running Dodger.

Jackie Robinson looks to the future.

Jackie Romps Home From Second Base As 26,000 Cheer

By WENDELL SMITH, Courier Sports Editor

EBBETS FIELD, Brooklyn, N. Y.—Here is the play by play account of the Brooklyn-Boston big league opener as played here Tuesday afternoon before a crowd of 26,623:

FIRST INNING

BOSTON—Culler grounded to third baseman Jorgensen who threw to ROBINSON for the putout. Hopp struck out. McCormick singled to center and went to second on a wild pitch. Elliott walked and then Litwhiler flied to center.

BROOKLYN—Stanky grounded out, second to first. ROBINSON grounded out, third to first. Reiser walked. Walker grounded out, pitcher to first.

SECOND INNING

BOSTON—Torgeson walked. Masi popped to Reese. Ryan hit into a fast double play, Stanky to Reese to ROBINSON.

BROOKLYN—Hermanski popped to second. Edwards flied deep to center. Jorgensen walked and Reese flied to right.

THIRD INNING

BOSTON—ROBINSON made all three putouts. Sain grounded out, third to first. Culler was out, short to first. Hopp went out, Stanky to ROBINSON.

Front page of the *Pittsburgh Courier* from April 19, 1947, shortly after Jackie Robinson broke Major League Baseball's color line. Under the management of editor and publisher Robert Lee Vann (1879–1940), the *Courier* was among the most widely circulated African American newspapers of the 1920s and 1930s. During the 1940s, the *Courier*'s influential sportswriter Wendell Smith encouraged big league teams to sign African-American ballplayers like Robinson, Larry Doby, and Satchel Paige.

pany newspaper, *The Guardian*. Part of the job involved collecting interesting stories from black newspapers and reprinting them in *The Guardian*. This gave Johnson the idea for a magazine similar to *Reader's Digest*, only for the black community. He called his magazine the *Negro Digest*.

The biggest problem Johnson faced was that no one wanted to lend him money to start the magazine. Finally, he was able to borrow $500. He used this to send out letters asking people to subscribe to the yet unpublished magazine for $2. From this he raised $6,000 and published his first issue in 1942.

In the beginning, the *Negro Digest* was not a great success. Then Johnson hit on the idea of asking famous white people to write an essay on "If I Were a Negro." When First Lady Eleanor Roosevelt sent in an essay, interest in the magazine exploded. Johnson was able to quit his job at Supreme Liberty Life Insurance and work full time at publishing.

Ebony was his next venture. He saw it as a black *Life* magazine. This time, he had plenty of people who wanted to subscribe, but no advertisers. Magazines and newspapers make most of their money from selling advertising. Without major advertisers, it cost Johnson more to print each copy of *Ebony* than he could sell it for. It took over a year before he could persuade large white companies such as Quaker Oats and Pepsi-Cola to advertise in *Ebony*.

Did You Know?

Alonzo Washington (b 1967), the creator of the African-American superhero Omega Man, uses his comics to send a positive message for social change. In his comics, African American superheroes fight crime, gangs, and drugs. Washington's company, Omega 7 Comics, is the most successful black-owned comic book company in the United States.

After *Ebony*, Johnson launched a magazine called *Tan*. This was followed by book publishing and a book club. Johnson and his wife, Eunice Walker Johnson, also started a hair care products company, a line of fashions, a travel agency, and Fashion Fair Cosmetics.

John Johnson was one of the most successful entrepreneurs of the twentieth century, but he still felt the sting of discrimination. He said that "no matter how much money you acquire or what sort of positions you hold, you're still black. And you're never free of that. . . . Now, when I step out of this building [his headquarters], I'm a black man. I'm not John Johnson, the publisher."

CATHERINE HUGHES AND RADIO ONE

Catherine Hughes (b. 1947) is the founder and chief executive officer (CEO) or "top boss" of Radio One. Radio One is the leading network for African-American radio programming. It has 54 stations across the United States. In 1996, *Black Enterprise* magazine named Hughes one of the 50 most powerful women in business.

Charlotta Bass and the Eagle

It is unusual for a black woman to own a newspaper, but for 40 years, Charlotta Bass (c.1880–1969) used her Los Angeles paper, the *California Eagle*, to fight for justice and equality for African Americans and women.

Bass was one of the pioneers of Civil Rights. She practiced advocacy journalism, meaning that she used her newspaper to write about events in a way that clearly told her readers how they should feel about issues and what they should do about them. Her paper spoke out about discrimination, unequal education, police brutality, the Ku Klux Klan, substandard housing, and the lack of jobs for blacks. For example, her paper urged black shoppers to boycott white businesses with the slogan "Don't shop where you can't work."

Bass was so outspoken that her life was threatened, and the FBI put her under surveillance because they were afraid that her writing would encourage African Americans to rise up against the government and rebel against authority. This did not stop Bass from speaking out. In 1951 Bass sold the *Eagle*, but she continued her activism and ran for vice president of the United States on the Independent Progressive Party ticket in 1952.

In 2011, a broadcast industry publication called *Radio Facts* ranked Cathy Hughes second (behind Oprah Winfrey) on its "Top 30 Black Women in Media" list.

The road that Hughes took out of an Omaha, Nebraska housing project to the top of a media empire was full of twists and obstacles. Hughes was the only African American at her Catholic girls' school. At 16 she became pregnant, married, and dropped out of school. She was divorced at age 18. Hughes could have become another dropout teen mother. Instead, she was inspired to make a better life for her son.

After taking classes to finish her education, Hughes became an administrative assistant to Tony Brown, founder of the communications department at Howard University. Through Brown, she got a job at the university radio station. Eventually she became the station's general manager. But when Hughes wanted to change the format to smooth love songs she called "The Quiet Storm," the university wasn't interested.

After Hughes remarried, she and her husband wanted to buy their own station. They went to 32 banks before they found one that would give them a loan. When Hughes and her husband divorced, she was left with a radio station but no money to run it. It took four years for the station to make a profit. After that, Hughes went on to acquire other radio stations and form Radio One.

Although she runs a successful business, Hughes has been criticized by both blacks and whites. Blacks have criticized her for putting profits ahead of community needs, while whites have criticized her for being too focused on black issues and concerns. Her trip from the projects to the boardroom highlights many of the obstacles African Americans in business have had to overcome time and time again.

The nationally syndicated *Oprah Winfrey Show* made Oprah Winfrey (b. 1945) a household name. Not content with being a talk show celebrity, Winfrey has become a corporate executive with a production company, a magazine, and in 2011, her own cable television channel, the Oprah Winfrey Network (OWN). Winfrey had a difficult childhood, but she rose above her hardships to become one of the most influential black businesswomen in the world.

7

BEHIND THE STARS
THE ENTERTAINMENT BUSINESS

Percy Ellis Sutton (1920–2010), a New York politician, lawyer, and radio station owner, proclaimed "black people must control elements in the news media in order to liberate themselves. We must begin to define ourselves, not always be defined by someone else."

The ability of African Americans to define themselves and promote their talents has perhaps best been achieved in the field of entertainment. In the past 50 years, black entertainers have become very successful and have largely been accepted by audience of all races. Behind the scenes, African-American businesspeople have supported them by managing their careers, promoting their music, or producing films or television programs for them to star in.

THOMAS BURRELL AND THE RISE OF BLACK ADVERTISING

Radio and television stations make their money by selling advertising. For years, white companies ignored African Americans as potential customers because most of them were poor. In the 1950s, blacks began to have more money to spend. But advertising was still aimed only at white customers. If blacks were used in advertisements, it usually was as maids or laborers. Thomas Burrell (b. 1939) changed that.

Burrell grew up in Englewood, a tough Chicago ghetto. He describes his youth this way. "I wasn't a good athlete, I wasn't a good gang fighter, I wasn't a good bike rider—I was outside every group and that's probably what saved me. Otherwise I'd probably be in Englewood, still hanging out." A high school aptitude test showed that Burrell was artistic and persuasive. A teacher suggested that although his grades were low, he might succeed in writing the words, or "copy," used in advertisements.

After flunking out of college and working in a factory, Burrell returned to college and worked part time in the mailroom of an advertising agency. While delivering mail, he heard that the creative department was having

Harry Pace and Black Swan Records

After failing at magazine publishing, Harry Herbert Pace (1884–1943) moved to Harlem, New York, where in 1921 he formed the first black-owned recording company, Pace Phonograph Corporation. In 1922 he renamed the company Black Swan Records, and set out to promote jazz and blues albums by the African-American artists he recorded. For a few years, Pace's company was a modest success. Black Swan marketed its albums directly to the African-American community, although some records did achieve mainstream success. Some of the performers who recorded on the label included Ethel Waters, Trixie Smith, and Bessie Allison.

Black Swan struggled financially after a few years, so in 1924 Pace sold the record label to a larger, white-owned record company, Paramount Records. Although Black Swan did not last long, it has been credited with showing the major record companies the appeal of African-American performers. Pace went on to found a successful life insurance company in Newark, New Jersey.

Thomas Burrell established the advertising agency Burrell Communications Group in 1971. The company, which has won numerous awards, specializes in the African-American market. It's goal, stated on the company's website, is to "consistently deliver creative, market-moving ideas." In 2011, Burrell Communications Group celebrated its 40th year in business.

trouble coming up with a good advertisement for a client. He went to the director and offered to help. The director gave him a chance to try. He was successful and soon became a copywriter.

In time, Burrell moved to larger advertising agencies. He eventually started his own firm. Burrell emphasized that African Americans are "not just dark-skinned white people." He meant that to be successful, advertisements directed at black consumers should celebrate the unique heritage and culture of African Americans. Burrell built his agency into a multi-million dollar business by creating advertisements for Coca-Cola, McDonalds, and other major corporations that spoke directly to the concerns and image of the black community.

BLACK MUSIC CROSSES OVER

Once radio stations realized the potential for advertising to African Americans, they began hire more black disc jockeys who played more

Motown Records founder Berry Gordy is a member of both the Rock and Roll Hall of Fame (inducted in 1988) and the Junior Achievement U.S. Business Hall of Fame (inducted 1998).

African-American artists. In 1947, 16 out of 3,000 disc jockeys were African American. By the mid-1950s there were 500 black DJs.

Radio programs that targeted the African American community gave black musicians the opportunity to be heard by more people. But the real breakthrough for black singers came when Berry Gordy's Motown began producing hit records in the early 1960s.

Berry Gordy, Jr. (b. 1929) was raised in Detroit. He dropped out of high school to become a professional boxer, but soon realized that he would never make a living boxing. Gordy was drafted into Army and served in Korea. On returning to Detroit, he opened a record store that quickly failed. To support his family, he went to work on the assembly line at Ford Motors. He spent his free time hanging around rhythm and blues (R&B) clubs and writing songs. Eventually, he succeeded in having some of his songs recorded. The record companies made big profits from his songs, but Gordy received only a little money for them. This gave him the idea of starting his own recording studio, which he called Motown Records.

Gordy teamed up with Smokey Robinson and the Miracles to release his first record in 1959. Robinson convinced Gordy it made financial sense to market his records himself instead of using larger companies to promote them. By 1961, Gordy and Robinson released "Shop Around." It was their major hit, selling more than a million copies.

The music of Motown Records was R&B-based (Gordy called it "ghetto music"), and was considered "black" music. Before the 1960s, pop music was considered "white" music. Gordy's great success came from breaking through this stereotype and having his music accepted by white audiences.

One way Gordy did this was to specialize in girl groups such as the Marvellettes, Martha Reeves and the Vandellas, and the Supremes. He controlled their image, dictating how they should dress, how they should act, and teaching them proper etiquette. Some of his singers resented this, but it made them more acceptable and less threatening to white audiences, and they were a huge success. Between 1964 and 1967, 114 Motown records reached number one on the pop charts and 20 records reached number one on the R&B charts.

FROM RADIO TO TELEVISION

In 1968, Berry Gordy hired an assistant named Suzanne de Passe (b. 1947). When Gordy met de Passe, she was booking acts into clubs in New York City. He was impressed with her ability to spot talent. Not only did de Passe discover Michael Jackson and the Jackson Five, she moved the Motown offices from Detroit to Los Angeles and took the company into television production. This was a good move, because musical tastes were changing and the smooth sound of Motown was giving way to a rougher, grittier musical sound.

In 1988, Gordy sold Motown Records, but kept the production company. Under de Passe's leadership, the company produced

Since leaving Motown, Suzanne de Passe has become a successful film and television producer.

During the 1980s Russell Simmons (b. 1957) was as successful in promoting hip-hop music to a diverse audience as Berry Gordy had been in taking R&B into the mainstream during the 1960s. The success of the record label Simmons helped to found, Def Jam Recordings, enabled the entrepreneur to expand into other businesses, including fashion and television production.

Lonesome Dove, a highly rated television miniseries. This was notable because *Lonesome Dove* was a Western, not a black-oriented story. De Passe went on to produce many television movies and series such as *Sister, Sister* and *Smart Guy*. In the 1990s, with Gordy retired, she changed the name of the production company to De Passe Productions.

CONQUERING CABLE TELEVISION

While Suzanne de Passe was moving toward television programming with mass appeal, Robert Johnson (b. 1946) was moving in the opposite direction. He created Black Entertainment Television (BET), a cable station that broadcasts only black-oriented programming.

Johnson was born in Mississippi and grew up in Illinois. He graduated from the University of Illinois and earned a master's degree from Princeton University. After working as a press aid for several elected officials in Washington D.C., he took a job as vice president of government relations for the National Cable and Television Association.

The major television networks broadcast almost no black-oriented programming in the 1970s. Johnson saw cable television, with its many channels and lower start-up costs, as a way to change this. He left his job and borrowed enough money to start BET as a cable channel in 1980.

It took ten years for BET to become financially successful, but in 1991 Johnson formed a parent company, BET Holdings, sold stock, and became the first black-owned corporation to be traded on the New York Stock Exchange.

Selling stock gave the company the money to acquire more programming, publish several magazines, and launch a pay movie channel.

The success of the Black Entertainment Television (BET) network made Robert L. Johnson the first African-American billionaire. Since selling the company, Johnson has started a new firm called The RLJ Companies, which owns businesses in a variety of fields, including publishing, automobile sales, financial management, and real estate investment.

Seven years later, Johnson converted BET into a private company and sold it to white-owned Viacom for $3 billion. Although this angered some blacks, the deal made Robert Johnson the first black billionaire. He has used his money become the principle owner of the National Basketball Association's Charlotte Hornets, another first for an African American.

CHAPTER NOTES

p. 9: "a place where Negro ladies . . ." quoted in Juliet E. K. Walker, *The History of Black Business in America* (New York: Macmillan, 1998), p. 214.

p. 11: "I have always believed . . ." S.B. Fuller, quoted in John M. Ingham and Lynne B. Feldman, *African-American Business Leaders: A Biographical Dictionary* (Westport, Conn.: Greenwood Press, 1994), p. 246.

p. 11: "lack of understanding..." Ibid., p. 248.

p. 15: "irresponsible men from attempting..." quoted in George E. Haynes, *The Negro at Work* (New York: AMS Press, 1968), p. 97.

p. 16: "the undisputed queen . . ." "Dining Out Guide: Where to Find Pies," *New York Times* (October 19, 1984). http://events.nytimes.com/mem/nycreview.html?_r=1&res=9B04EED61739F93AA25753C1A962948260&scp=4&sq=sylvia%20woods%20queen%20of%20soul%20food&st=cse

p. 18: "it was not rare . . ." Walker, *The History of Black Business in America*, p. 255.

p. 21: "will take nickels . . ." Maggie Walker quoted in Ingham and Feldman, *African-American Business Leaders: A Biographical Dictionary*, p.674.

p. 22: "because of social diseases . . ." quoted in J. H. Harmon, Arnett Lindsey, and Carter G. Woodson, *Negro as a Business Man* (College Park, Md.: McGrath Publishing Co., 1969), p.96.

p. 23: "whites simply don't trade . . ." A. M. Walker, quoted in Ingham and Feldman, *African-American Business Leaders: A Biographical Dictionary,* p.664.

p. 24: "We had little . . ." Stanley O'Neal, quoted in Eric Weiner, "Stan O'Neal: The Rise and Fall of a Numbers Guy." National Public Radio broadcast, October 29, 2007. http://www.npr.org/templates/story/story.php?storyId=15738661

p. 26: "A big black man . . ." Sarah Breedlove, quoted in Ingham and Feldman, *African-American Business Leaders: A Biographical Dictionary,* p.682.

p. 26: "People would want . . ." Marjorie Joiner, quoted in Ingham and Feldman, *African-American Business Leaders: A Biographical Dictionary*, p.686.

p. 28: "business is business . . ." C. H. James, quoted in Ingham and Feldman, *African-American Business Leaders: A Biographical Dictionary,* p.341.

p. 30: "the superstar of cookies . . ." Wallace Amos, quoted in Ingham and Feldman, *African-American Business Leaders: A Biographical Dictionary,* p.28.

p. 33: "an example of thrift and self-government." Booker T. Washington, "A Town Owned by Negroes," *The World's Work* vol. 14 (July 1907), p. 9125.

p. 40: "a little too dark . . ." quoted in Ingham and Feldman, *African-American Business Leaders: A Biographical Dictionary,* p. 4.

p. 41: "show not only white people . . ." John H. Johnson, quoted in Ingham and Feldman, *African-American Business Leaders: A Biographical Dictionary*, p. 372.

p. 43: "no matter how much money . . ." Ibid., p. 377.

p. 47: "black people must control . . ." Percy Sutton, quoted in Ingham and Feldman, *African-American Business Leaders: A Biographical Dictionary*, p. 610.

p. 48: "I wasn't a good athlete . . ." Thomas Burrell, quoted in Ingham and Feldman, *African-American Business Leaders: A Biographical Dictionary*, p. 121.

p. 49: "consistently deliver creative, market-moving ideas," Burrell Communications Group, "Our Approach," http://burrell.com/company/our-approach.

p. 49: "not just dark-skinned . . ." Thomas Burrell, quoted in Ingham and Feldman, *African-American Business Leaders: A Biographical Dictionary*, p. 124.

GLOSSARY

ambassador—an important diplomat who officially represents his country to the government of foreign country.

catering—a business that provides food and drink and sometimes tables, chairs, and accessories for an event. In the 1870s wealthy people often had dinner parties and dances catered at their homes. Today caterers are more likely to provide food for weddings, parties, and business events held in public places such as hotels and conference centers.

chaplain—a religious leader who ministers to members of an institution such as the Army, a school, or a prison.

chief executive officer (CEO)—usually the top boss of a company. The CEO is in charge of total management of the business.

copywriter—a person who generates creative ideas for and writes advertisements.

domestic service—working as a maid, cook, or housecleaner in another person's home.

foreclosure—the legal process that allows a bank that has loaned money to build houses or buy property to take possession of the property when the loan is not repaid on time. The bank then sells the property to someone else.

Great Depression—a period or economic crisis and hardship beginning with the stock market crash in 1929 and lasting through most of the 1930s. During this time, about one-third of all American workers were unable to find jobs and many businesses went bankrupt.

Great Migration—the movement of more than 4 million African Americans from the rural South to cities in the North.

invest—to use money to buy something or make loans that you expect will increase in value.

mortgage—a legal contract that allows a person to borrow money to buy a property and pay the loan back over time. The borrower must pay back the amount borrowed plus an extra agreed-upon amount called interest within a specific time.

NAACP—National Association for the Advancement of Colored People, an organization founded in 1909 to work for equality of opportunity for people of color and to eliminate discrimination based on race.

speculator—a person who buys goods or property for a low price in the hope of being able to sell it at a much higher price.

steward—a person who is in charge of buying food and managing dining arrangements.

temperance movement—a social movement that was against drinking of alcohol because of its negative effects on individuals, families, and communities. It began in the United States in the early 1800s and ended with the passage of the Eighteenth Amendment to the Constitution, which prohibited the manufacture, transportation, and use of alcohol. In 1933, the Twenty-first Amendment to the Constitution repealed (undid) the Eighteenth Amendment, and alcohol once again became legal to make and use in the United States.

Wall Street—a street in New York City where the New York Stock Exchange is located. Wall Street is considered the center of American financial businesses. Wall Street businesses are those involved with trading stocks, bonds, commodities such as gold and oil, and generally investing and managing money.

FURTHER READING

Buckley, Annie. *Robert L Johnson*. Ann Arbor, Mich.: Cherry Lake Publishing, 2007.

Harris, Lanzen, ed. *Biography for Beginners: African American Leaders*. Pleasant Ridge, MI: Favorable Impressions, 2007

Haskins, Jim. *African American Entrepreneurs*. New York: John Wiley & Sons, 1998.

Ingram, John M., and Lynne B. Feldman. *African-American Business Leaders: A Biographical Dictionary*. Westport, Conn.: Greenwood Press, 1994

Kranz, Rachel. *African-American Business Leaders and Entrepreneurs*. New York: Facts on File, 2004.

Lies, Anne. *Oprah Winfrey: Media Mogul*. Minneapolis: Abdo Publishing Co., 2011.

Walker, Juliet E. K. *The History of Black Business in America*. New York: Macmillan, 1998.

INTERNET RESOURCES

http://www.cr.nps.gov/nr/twhp/wwwlps/lessons/53black/53black.htm

Chicago's Black Metropolis traces the history of Chicago with emphasis on the development of African American businesses.

http://www.themsj.com/black-business-leaders-in-america-1.2440240#.T1qRGfVXljs

The *Monroe Street Journal*, the official newspaper of the Stephen M. Ross School of Business at the University of Michigan, has an article "Black Business Leaders in America: Moving Markets and Creating Industries," that profiles four contemporary African American business leaders.

http://www.smallbizchicago.com/2011/02/black-business-leaders-blast-stubborn-stereotypes-despite-success

An article from *Small Business Chicago* about how black business leaders are still stereotyped.

http://www.h-net.org/~business/bhcweb/publications/BEHprint/v022n1/p0262-p0272.pdf

Scholarly article on African-American business leaders in the South from 1810 to 1945.

http://afrimoney.com/famous-african-american-business-leaders.php

Links to famous African-American business leaders' blogs.

INDEX

Abbott, Robert Sengstacke, 39–41
advertising businesses, 47–49
affirmative action programs, 12
African American businesses, 9–13
  and African American customers, ***8***, 9, 10–11, 13, 17–18, 23, 25
  entertainment, 47–53
  financial, 19–24
  media, ***38***, 39–45, ***46***, 52–53
  real estate, 31, 33–37
  sales, 25–30
  service, 13–18
  and white customers, 11, 17, 23, 28
African American women
  and banking, 21–22
  and media, 44–45, ***46***
  and sales, 25–27, 29
  and service businesses, 13–14, 16, 17, 18
Afro-American Realty Company, 36, 37
Allensworth, Allen, 34
Amos, Wallace, 29–30

banking businesses, 19–22, 23, 36
Baptiste, Amelia, 15
Bass, Charlotta, 44
Binga, Jesse, 36
Black Enterprise, 27, 41, 44
Black Entertainment Television (BET), 52–53
Black Swan Records, 48
Bragg, Janet, 17
Breedlove, Sarah (Madame C.J. Walker). *See* Walker, Madame C.J.
Brown, Tony, 45
Browne, William Washington, 20–21
burial societies, 19
  See also insurance businesses
Burrell, Thomas, 47–49
businesses. *See* African American businesses

Cain, Herman, ***12***
California Eagle (newspaper), 44
Caterers Manufacturing and Supply Company, 15
Chappell, Emma, 22
Chenault, Kenneth, 24
Chicago Defender (newspaper), ***38***, 39–41
Civil Rights Movement, 10–12, 15, 18, 24, 44
Civil War, 9, 13, 14, 19, 33
Coleman, Warren C., ***10***
Consolidated Bank and Trust Company, 22
cosmetics businesses, 25–26, 27, 43
  See also sales businesses
Cox, Wayne, 23

Davis, Joseph, 31, 33
De Passe, Suzanne, 51–52
Delta Penny Savings Bank, 23
discrimination, 9, 11, 23, 24, 33, 37
Downing, George T., 15
Dutrieuille, Albert, 15
Dutrieuille, Peter Albert, 14–15

Ebony Magazine, 41, 43
entertainment businesses, 47–53

Famous Amos Cookies, 29–30
financial businesses, 19–24
Fletcher, Alphonse, Jr., 24
Fletcher Asset Management, 24
Franklin, C.W., ***14***
Freedman's Savings and Trust, 19–20
Fuller, S.B., 11
funeral homes, 13–14
  See also service businesses

Geddes, Clem, 14
Gordy, Berry, 50–52
Graves, Earl, 41
Great Depression, 10, 29
Great Migration, 9, 36
Green, Ben, 33
Green, Victor H., ***18***

hair care businesses. *See* cosmetics businesses
Harlem, New York City, ***8***, 16, ***20***, 34–37
home ownership, 31, 37
hospitality businesses, 14–18
  See also service businesses

Numbers in ***bold italics*** refer to captions.

Hughes, Catherine, 44–45

insurance businesses, 19, 22–23

James, Charles Howell, 28
James, Edward, 28–29
James Produce Company, 27–29
Jefferson, Lucy, 13
John, Daymond, ***12***
Johnson, Eunice Walker, 43
Johnson, George, 27
Johnson, John Harold, 41, 43–44
Johnson, Reverdy, 17
Johnson, Robert, 52–53
Johnson, William, 13

manufacturing businesses, ***10***, 25, 26, 27
media businesses, ***38***, 39–45, ***46***, 52–53
Mississippi Life Insurance Company, 23
Montgomery, Benjamin, 31, 33
Montgomery, Isaiah, 31, 33
Motown Records, 50–52
Mound Bayou, Mississippi, 32, 33–34
music businesses, 49–52
mutual aid societies, 19, 20–21, 22
See also banking businesses; insurance businesses

Nail, John, 37
Naomi Sims Beauty Products, 29
Negro Digest, 43

Omega 7 Comics, 43
O'Neal, Stanley, 24
Overton, Anthony, 27

Pace, Harry Herbert, 48
Pace Phonograph Corporation. *See* Black Swan Records
Parker, Henry, 37
Payne, William, 34
Payton, Philip, 35–37

Radio One, 44, 45
real estate businesses, 31, 33–37
redlining, 37
RLJ Companies, ***53***
Roosevelt, Eleanor, 43

sales businesses, 25–30
segregation, 9, 10, 17–18, 24, 36
Sengstacke, John, 41
Sengstacke, Robert, 39
service businesses, 13–18
Simmons, Russell, ***52***
Sims, Naomi, 29
Smith, Wendell, ***42***
St. Luke Penny Savings Bank, 21–22
Sutton, Percy Ellis, 47
Sylvia's Restaurant, 16

Tri-State Bank, 23
Turnbo-Malone, Annie, 27

United Bank of Philadelphia, 22
United Order of the True Reformers, 20–21
Universal Life Insurance Company, 23

Vann, Robert Lee, ***42***

W. H. Johnson Funeral Home, 13
Walker, Antonio Maceo, 23
Walker, C.J., 26
Walker, Joseph Edison, 22–23
Walker, Madame C.J., 25–26, 27, 37
Walker, Maggie Lena, 21–22
Walker, Sally, 18
Washington, Alonzo, 43
Washington, Booker T., 34
Washington, Sarah, 26–27
Willis, Gertrude Geddes, 14
Winfrey, Oprah, ***45***, ***46***
Woods, Sylvia, 16
Wormley, James, 15, 17

CONTRIBUTORS

Tish Davidson has written many articles for newspapers and magazines. Her books for middle school readers include *School Conflict, Prejudice, and Facing Competition*. She was chosen a California Readers author of the month for September 2010. Davidson lives in Fremont, California and is a volunteer puppy raiser for Guide Dogs for the Blind.

Senior Consulting Editor **Dr. Marc Lamont Hill** is one of the leading hip-hop generation intellectuals in the country. Dr. Hill has lectured widely and provides regular commentary for media outlets like NPR, the *Washington Post*, *Essence Magazine*, the *New York Times*, CNN, MSNBC, and *The O'Reilly Factor*. He is the host of the nationally syndicated television show *Our World With Black Enterprise*. Dr. Hill is a columnist and editor-at-large for the *Philadelphia Daily News*. His books include the award-winning *Beats, Rhymes, and Classroom Life: Hip-Hop Pedagogy and the Politics of Identity* (2009).

Since 2009 Dr. Hill has been on the faculty of Columbia University as Associate Professor of Education at Teachers College. He holds an affiliated faculty appointment in African American Studies at the Institute for Research in African American Studies at Columbia University.

Since his days as a youth in Philadelphia, Dr. Hill has been a social justice activist and organizer. He is a founding board member of My5th, a non-profit organization devoted to educating youth about their legal rights and responsibilities. He is also a board member and organizer of the Philadelphia Student Union. Dr. Hill also works closely with the ACLU Drug Reform Project, focusing on drug informant policy. In addition to his political work, Dr. Hill continues to work directly with African American and Latino youth.

In 2005, *Ebony* named Dr. Hill one of America's 100 most influential Black leaders. The magazine had previously named him one of America's top 30 Black leaders under 30 years old.